W9-ASN-969

Dearly, Nearly, Insincerely

What Is an Adverb?

To Elio, Gina, and Vince who get
along swimmingly   —B.P.C.

For Sari   —B.G.

Adverb: A word
that describes
when, how, where,
how often, and
how much.

Dearly, Nearly, Insincerely

What Is an Adverb?

by Brian P. Cleary

illustrated by Brian Gable

M MILLBROOK PRESS / MINNEAPOLIS

Adverbs tell us when and how,

Like, quickly do your homework, now.

They often help describe the verbs,

Like, **patiently** plant
peas and herbs.

PEAS

AdVerbs add character,
sizzle, and fizz

To your phrase or your
sentence, whatever it is!

Frankly, this hot dog just couldn't be better.

Sheepishly, Fred found he'd ruined his sweater.

If they tell us **how,**
they're an
"adverb of manner,"

Like, slowly this summer,
my sister got tanner.

"Frequency adverbs"
will tell us how often,

Like, seldom
have I seen
a lovelier coffin.

They give us a time,
a place, and
a number,

Like, yesterday, over there,
I was in slumber.

First, I was tired,

then, I was woozy,

Next, I began feeling sleepy and snoozy.

They modify **adVerbs**, like, she sang quite nicely.

Or he speaks so swiftly but Very precisely.

Presently, pleasantly, properly praise.

Speedily, sometimes quite greedily, graze.

Curiously, furiously,
strikingly strong,

Helplessly lost and
hopelessly wrong.

Adverbs, you'll find,
give the adjectives zip!

As in foolishly frisky

and
famously hip—

Bitterly angry, bitingly cold,

Brilliantly burgundy, shockingly old.

The adjective's "good,"
the **adverb** is "well."

So now that
you know that,
you're able to tell

That well's how you felt,
and good was your day.

Yes, Well is a
Very deep subject,
I'd say!

Truly, deeply,
Sadly, badly—

I tell you these are
adVerbs, gladly.

And so are
sleekly and
uniquely,

Bravely,
boldly,

coldly, meekly.

So, what is an **adVerb?**

Do you know?

ABOUT THE AUTHOR & ILLUSTRATOR

BRIAN P. CLEARY is the author of the Words Are CATegorical©, Math Is CATegorical©, Food Is CATegorical™, Adventures in Memory™, and Sounds Like Reading™ series. He has also written The Laugh Stand: Adventures in Humor; Peanut Butter and Jellyfishes: A Very Silly Alphabet Book; The Punctuation Station; and two poetry books. Mr. Cleary lives in Cleveland, Ohio.

BRIAN GABLE is the illustrator of several Words Are CATegorical© books, as well as the Math Is CATegorical© series. Mr. Gable also works as a political cartoonist for the Globe and Mail newspaper in Toronto, Canada.

Text copyright © 2003 by Brian P. Cleary
Illustrations copyright © 2003 by Lerner Publishing Group, Inc.

Millbrook Press, a division of Lerner Publishing Group, Inc.
241 First Avenue North, Minneapolis, MN 55401 U.S.A.

Website address: www.lernerbooks.com

Library of Congress Cataloging-in-Publication Data

Cleary, Brian P., 1959—
    Dearly, nearly, insincerely : what is an adverb? / by Brian P. Cleary;
    illustrated by Brian Gable.
        p.   cm. — (Words are categorical)
    Summary: Rhyming text and illustrations present numerous examples of
    adverbs and their functions.
        ISBN-13: 978—0—87614—924—9 (lib. bdg. : alk. paper)
        ISBN-10: 0—87614—924—7 (lib. bdg. : alk. paper)
        1. English language—Adverb—Juvenile literature. [1. English language—
    Adverb.] I. Gable, Brian, 1949— II. Title.
    PE1325 .C57 2003
    428.2—dc21   2002003012

Manufactured in the United States of America
13 — DP — 11/1/10